BE COOL & CONFIDENT

A GUIDE FOR GUYS

BE COOL & CONFIDENT

A GUIDE FOR GUYS

WYNNE DALLEY

tell me

New Haven, Connecticut

Library of Congress Control Number 2013930565
ISBN 978-0-9816453-5-3 (softcover)
ISBN 978-0-9829421-7-8 (e-book)

Illustrations by Ted Enik
Model (pp 39-40): Luis Ramirez III
Photographer (pp 39-40): Ronni Anderson
Cover design by Linda Loiewski

Printed in the United States of America
First edition
10 9 8 7 6 5 4 3 2 1

Distribution by Greenleaf Book Group LLC

tell me
Published by **Tell Me Press**
98 Mansfield St.
New Haven, CT 06511
www.tellmepress.com

FOR MAX, ADAM, AND BEN

FOR MAX, ADAM, AND BEN

CONTENTS

CONTENTS

ACKNOWLEDGMENTS

Thanks to Reed, who was a true gentleman; Eve and Leslie Kark, who raised the standard of kindness and courtesy; Fred, William, and Charlie, very cool young men; Luis Ramirez, for demonstrating the correct way to tie a tie; Teo Tertel, for his invaluable help on both books; Scott Williams, for his wisdom; Russ Fischella, for taking great photographs; and Jack, for his love and support.

Thanks to my family and friends for their loyal support and genuine enthusiasm for my belief in helping teens feel confident and cool.

INTRODUCTION

Although my career as a model agent and a modeling school director was primarily focused on girls and young women, there were times, particularly in the glamorous world of fashion photography, when young men were involved. It became clear that training in good manners and the importance of grooming was essential for boys, too. Even if you're not in the modeling profession, this still holds true, no matter what your career choice ends up being. Why not use to your advantage methods that work for highly paid professionals? Being friendly, courteous, polite, and well-mannered, as well as paying attention to your appearance and grooming, will always be a plus.

My message to young people, both boys and girls, has always been the same. Make the best of yourself. Never neglect your health, your appearance, your education, or your self-esteem. The most worthwhile thing you can do in life, and particularly during your teen years, is to invest in yourself. Good manners and a well-groomed appearance show the world you have respect for yourself and those around you.

In this guide you will learn the basics of good manners: a clean appearance, a positive attitude, how to interact with adults in a charming way, and other important social tips.

Being polite is not nerdy. Good manners really *are* cool!

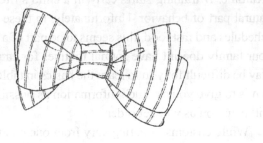

CHAPTER 1

TABLE MANNERS

You may look around at your friends and ask, "Why should I be the only one with good manners?" Correct table manners are essential. It immediately tells people that you understand how to behave in social situations with ease and confidence. On the plus side, girls like to see boys behaving politely.

We all deserve to enjoy a meal, whether it is at home or at a restaurant, without the embarrassment of watching someone who does not know, or care, about correct table manners. Eating a good meal should not be a "race against time"; it should be savored and not be an ugly experience for those around you. Sit up straight, take your time, and listen to what others have to say.

Traditionally, table manners were taught by parents at every mealtime. If training starts early in a child's life, it becomes a natural part of behavior. Unfortunately, in these days of hectic schedules and fast food, this seems to be part of a bygone age. If your family doesn't have formal routines for eating together, it may be difficult for you to learn the basics in table manners. My aim is to give you as much information as possible now, which will help you as you get older.

While customs of eating vary from one country to another, and the use of silverware, napkins, and utensils may change in position or use, good eating habits, regardless of culture, should be universal. Table manners must not be pretentious or phony. We should not have one set of rules for home and one for dining out, as this only causes confusion. On the other hand, it is important for you to know when a little extra effort is called for to show respect to those around you.

For example, if relatives are visiting from out of town (perhaps coming especially to see you), then it would make a very good impression for you to behave well. Greet them with enthusiasm and look clean and tidy. Pay attention to what they have to say, and maybe show them your latest projects. The worst thing would be for you to stay glued to your computer, cell phone, or television.

If your family is planning a special meal at home or at a restaurant in honor of visitors, this would be the perfect time for you to start behaving like a gentleman. Holding a chair back for a lady (such as your mother, an aunt, or your grandmother) is a nice touch and will make your parents proud. You don't need to make a fuss about it; just pull the chair back and stand by while the lady sits down. In a restaurant it is polite to let girls and ladies order from the menu first; when everyone is served, wait for the ladies to start eating before you do. These are little things to remember, but if you behave like this on a regular basis, good manners will become a habit.

Obviously if you are going out with a group of friends to get pizza or burgers, you can relax a few rules and go along with the fun. *Good manners never mean not having a good time.* However, by practicing good manners, when that special occasion comes along you will be prepared and know the right thing to do.

AT THE TABLE

In a formal dining situation, when everyone is invited to sit down by the host or hostess, it is important for men (including young men) to stay standing until the ladies sit down. Even if the host insists that everyone should sit down, you should be aware of who will be sitting next to you. If it's a lady or a girl, you should wait until she's seated before sitting down yourself.

If the lady is to your right, it is good manners to help her be seated by standing back and holding her chair for her. When you are both seated, please don't sit there looking bored. You may feel shy, but try to start a conversation. This will help everyone feel less awkward and make her more relaxed. If you can put yourself in someone else's place by easing the situation, you will be doing a good job.

Sit up straight with your hands in your lap. Never put your elbows on the table while eating or put your arm around the back of another person's chair. Keep elbows to your sides. This is not uncomfortable—it is correct and looks well mannered. When everyone has finished eating and plates are cleared, it is acceptable to rest elbows on the table while having a conversation.

Never start eating before the host or hostess, and if your mother, grandmother, or aunt is joining you at the table, wait for them to begin eating if you can. Sometimes this is not practical, but as a general rule, try to *hold back before digging in*, especially where girls are concerned.

When you do begin to eat, take small portions of food—not great mouthfuls. This looks ugly, and you could choke. Lean over your plate, so if food drops off the fork, it will land on your plate and not in your lap.

NAPKINS

The napkin will traditionally be on your left, on the bread plate or beside it. Sometimes at a formal dinner, napkins are folded in a wine glass or designed in an attractive shape on the dinner plate. Wherever the napkin is located, place it on your lap when you sit down.

When wiping your mouth with a napkin, always have your knife and fork in the "rest" position on your plate. (See "Which Knife and Fork?!" for a description.) It is wrong to hold a knife or fork while wiping your mouth. Never tuck your napkin into a collar or tie it around your neck (unless you are dining in a restaurant serving cracked crab or other shellfish to be eaten with the fingers). At the end of a meal, it is not necessary to fold your napkin; simply place it on the table to the left of your plate or beside the bread plate. If you have to get up and leave the table, you can place your napkin to the left of your bread plate or on the seat of your chair until you return. (If you are getting up to go to the restroom, you don't need to announce that. Simply remember to say "excuse me" and quietly leave the table.)

WHICH KNIFE AND FORK?!

There is a simple rule regarding the use of flatware or silverware: knives and forks are always placed in the order in which they will be used, from the outside moving in. Therefore, when you are faced with what might seem an endless display of cutlery in a restaurant or at a special dinner, don't be confused.

The soup spoon will be on your far right, and next will be the small salad knife or butter knife (or this might be placed across the bread and butter plate). The entrée knife is next, closest to the plate. On the left side of the plate, starting from the inside out, is the entrée fork, then the salad fork.

So knives are on the right, with matching forks on the left, in order of their use (working from right to left for the knives and left to right for the forks). Normally the dessert spoon

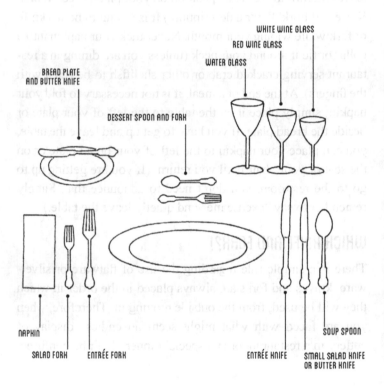

WHITE WINE GLASS

RED WINE GLASS

WATER GLASS

BREAD PLATE
AND BUTTER KNIFE

DESSERT SPOON AND FORK

NAPKIN

SALAD FORK   ENTRÉE FORK

ENTRÉE KNIFE   SMALL SALAD KNIFE
OR BUTTER KNIFE

SOUP SPOON

and fork are placed above the plate, the spoon above the fork. Occasionally a dessert spoon/fork will be brought in with the dessert, but normally it is on the table along with the other utensils. The method I have just explained is the correct and simplest form of placing and using silverware, although there are often slight variations, depending on the number of courses to be eaten, or depending on the customs and traditions of the host. When you are in doubt, follow the lead of the host and the others at your table.

Now that you know what goes where, what do you do—or *not* do? Never point a knife or fork at someone. Never hold the knife in the left hand to cut meat or any other food—this is a huge don't, and eating this way will make you look foolish and uneducated. Your knife should never be more than a few inches above your plate. Once you've used your utensils, they should not be placed back on the table. Instead, arrange them in the "rest" position by placing the knife and fork on your plate.

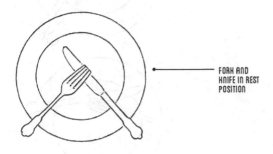

FORK AND
KNIFE IN REST
POSITION

The knife should be positioned with the sharp edge facing left. Practice the rest position so that it becomes a natural, easy thing to do. It's good manners to slow down during a meal, and it also signals to your server that you're not ready for your plate to be taken away. If a waiter or another helper in the restaurant wants to remove your plate, politely tell that person you're not finished, and pick up your knife and fork to continue eating.

The water glass and glasses for red and white wine are usually placed to the right, above the place setting. (Servers will remove the wineglasses for children or adults who choose not to drink wine.) Never hold the fork in one hand while your glass is in the other; put it down in the rest position along with your knife.

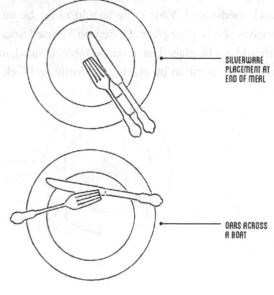

SILVERWARE
PLACEMENT AT
END OF MEAL

OARS ACROSS
A BOAT

When you have finished eating, place the silverware together on your plate parallel to one another. This will indicate to your server or host that you are finished. Never leave your knife and fork crossed like oars on a boat.

It may seem a lot to learn now, but practice will help. I always suggest to girls and boys that they go through this procedure a few times at home with table settings in order to feel at ease when that special meal or party comes along. The main purpose of entertaining or dining is to have a good time. Once you have figured out a few basic rules, you can then sit back, enjoy the food, enjoy the conversation, and enjoy the time with friends and family.

Remember, if you make a mistake, it is not the end of the world—keep eating, and don't draw attention to what you may think is an embarrassing "goof." Be cool, and instead focus on making conversation with those on either side of you. People are more interested in what you have to say than what fork you're using. In the grand scheme of things, using the wrong piece of cutlery is no big deal. Feeling at ease is much more important. The way you handle yourself will earn the respect of everyone around you.

BREAD AND CRACKERS

When eating dinner rolls, bread, or crackers, break off *small pieces*. Place a pat of butter on the side of your bread plate. Always break bread with your fingers on the bread plate.

Do not cut bread or rolls with the butter knife or spread a large piece of bread with butter. Instead, spread a little butter onto the individual pieces of bread to be eaten. This way of eating bread is simple and polite, and it becomes a habit very quickly if you practice. No more spreading butter on a whole slice of bread, especially at a formal dinner—leave that method for breakfast (when it is perfectly acceptable to spread butter or jam on a large slice of bread) and other meals at home. Otherwise, for more formal dining you should break small pieces of bread or crackers and butter each one separately.

SOUP

When eating soup, the soup spoon should be held in the right hand, with the thumb on top. As you fill the spoon with soup, be sure to move the spoon away from you, never toward you, since this will avoid spills on your clothes. (Makes sense, doesn't it? Most rules of etiquette are based on common sense like this and are not designed to make people nervous.) Sip soup from the side of the spoon, and never put the whole spoon in your mouth. If you sip slowly and tip the spoon slightly toward your mouth, you'll avoid slurping, which is rude and embarrassing. When you take a break, always rest the soup spoon on the plate underneath the soup dish—never back in the soup bowl. A bowl of soup is always served on its own plate for this reason.

MEAT

When eating meat, hold the fork in your left hand and cut small pieces, *one* piece at a time. (Do not cut all the meat at once.)

You may then place the fork in your right hand to eat (or keep it in the left if you are left-handed). Most Europeans, however, eat their food with the fork in the left hand; it's just a matter of custom. Either way, always have the prongs of the fork facing down. Once again, never cut your meat with the knife in your left hand and the fork in your right. You should never hold the knife in the left hand.

Small amounts of potatoes and vegetables may be placed on the fork with the meat, but keep it to a minimum. Never use your fork to scoop up vegetables as though you were using a spoon.

If you discover that you have a bone in your mouth, this can be removed by calmly lifting your napkin to your mouth and placing the bone inside. A small piece of meat that you cannot swallow can be placed onto your fork and put on the side of the plate. Similarly, a cherry pit from a dessert should be placed onto the dessert spoon or fork and left at the side of the dish.

WHAT TO EAT WITH YOUR FINGERS

Corn on the cob, asparagus, and artichoke leaves are eaten with the fingers. When you reach the heart of the artichoke, however, use your knife and fork. Chicken legs should not be eaten with fingers at a formal dinner, but it is acceptable at home or at a picnic. A crispy piece of bacon may be picked up as long as you behave with ease and confidence. Use common sense. Pizza, hamburgers, hot dogs, and other fast foods are typically eaten with your fingers, but be aware of the amount of food you put into your mouth—and use lots of napkins! Observing how polite adults around you are eating their food is a good way to learn how to behave in different situations.

DO'S AND DON'TS

- *Do* hold the chair for the lady to your right, and make conversation with her after you're both seated.

- *Do* wait for the host, and the ladies at the table, to begin eating before you start.

- *Do* eat calmly and slowly.

- *Do* tell the host how wonderful the food is.

- *Do* contribute to the conversation and remember to be a good listener.

- *Do* enjoy yourself. Having a meal with friends and family can be a wonderful time to relax, discover different foods, and hear a few good stories!

- *Don't* ever come to the table with your hat on. This shows a lack of respect. Don't forget to collect your hat when you leave the table (it would be expensive to keep buying hats!), but make sure you do not put it back on your head until you are outside.

- *Don't* put your elbows on the table while eating. It looks sloppy and disrespectful. You may, however, rest your elbows on the table when not eating or while having a conversation.

- *Don't* leave your spoon in the coffee cup. Rest it on the saucer.

- *Don't* put too much food into your mouth at once—it is very ugly and unappetizing—and don't chew with your mouth open or speak with your mouth full.

- *Don't* eat chicken with your fingers at the table—save that for a barbecue.

- *Don't* dive for a knife or fork if you accidentally drop it on the floor. Just pick up another utensil and continue eating.

- *Don't* slouch, and don't tilt your chair back. You could fall on the ground, and that would make you feel uncool.

- *Don't* leave the table without first asking for permission or saying "excuse me." (If you're leaving to use the bathroom, you don't need to say so.)

CHAPTER 2

A WELL-GROOMED
APPEARANCE

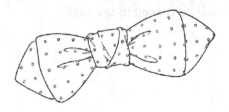

All animals need grooming. Horse lovers groom horses, cats groom themselves, chimpanzees groom each other, and dogs typically run and hide at the mention of "bath time." Although children love to play in the mud when they are young, as they mature they learn that looking clean and well groomed helps them feel more confident. You are growing up now, so overall cleanliness and general grooming habits should be kept up at all times since appearance is such a big part of making a good first impression—it is often the only information we have when we meet one another for the first time.

According to research done by psychologists, sometimes people who are considered physically attractive are given a head start and better treatment by others because they are thought to be more intelligent, kinder, or more sincere. This attitude is obviously unfair and not true. However, we are constantly being judged by others whether we like it or not, so it is in your best interest to learn how to go about improving certain aspects of your appearance and behavior. Of course, cleanliness is the number-one priority.

PERSONAL HYGIENE AND GROOMING

Teenagers, both boys and girls, should always be aware of personal hygiene, and, it goes without saying, they should shower every morning and use antiperspirant daily. After sports or other times when your body perspires, you would obviously shower again. There are some very good body-care products available, some made specifically for men (and boys), but any type of personal hygiene products will do. If you prefer to use a men's cologne or body spray after showering, please be aware that some people are sensitive to scents, so use sparingly, especially in hot weather. Basic soap, shampoo, and deodorant won't break the bank, but if you're concerned about the cost, an after-school job can help. Generally speaking, having a clean appearance doesn't have to be expensive.

It is not necessary to spend money on new clothes to look good. As long as they are clean and in good shape, that is all that's important. This sends a message to people that you have pride in your appearance. Once you get into the habit of wearing fresh, clean clothes, it will give you a feeling of positive self-esteem. Help out with the laundry chores once in a while. Your parents will appreciate it.

You are clean and clothed, but there's still more to consider, such as your hair. Speak to a professional barber or hairdresser about the right style for your individual features, taking into account the shape of your face and type of hair. Hair always looks better when it is well cut. Also, don't forget about your fingernails. They should be short and clean. If there are rough edges, smooth them out with a nail file.

Lastly, always carry a handkerchief or folded tissues, especially if you have a cold. A gentleman always carries these in his pocket. A sudden sneeze can take everyone by surprise, and hands are no substitute for tissues. Sneezing around people is not cool. Try to turn away if caught off guard, but rule number one is to be prepared. If a sneeze is unavoidable and you have no tissues or handkerchief, wash your hands as soon as possible to avoid spreading germs. Girls are easily put off by someone who acts in an immature way, and not having a handkerchief or tissue in your pocket is definitely immature.

With a clean body, fresh clothes (not necessarily new clothes), groomed fingernails, and a handkerchief or tissues in your pocket, you are well on your way to being in charge of your personal appearance. This will help you to become a cool dude!

SKIN CARE

You are clean and fresh, but showering has made your skin dry and rough. To prevent this, everyone should use a skin-softening lotion after bathing, as well as sunscreen daily. Research has shown that the sun's ultraviolet rays are the most damaging single factor in premature aging and skin cancer. Early facial wrinkles and damaged skin can be the result of too much sun, so start protecting your skin with sunscreen or sunblock now.

What's the difference? Sunscreens contain chemicals that absorb harmful rays, while sunblocks act as physical barriers by reflecting the rays. Many good sunscreens contain PABA (para-aminobenzoic acid), but no single preparation prevents all the sun's rays from penetrating the skin. There are also PABA-free sunscreens available for those who are allergic or sensitive. If you are concerned about acne, there are oil-free sunblocks available that will not clog pores. A lightweight, nongreasy, and waterproof lotion is an excellent choice. My advice would be to consult a dermatologist if you have very fair or sensitive skin to make sure you are using the correct product.

Everyone should apply a protective lotion, whether it be sunscreen or sunblock, when they are at the beach or the pool, as no one is immune to sunburn. While fair-skinned people are extremely vulnerable to burning, dark-skinned people are just as likely to suffer sunburn. On your first day at the beach or pool, don't lie out for hours under a hot sun. The sun's rays are strongest between ten in the morning and two in the afternoon. Most people don't realize that even under an umbrella they are exposed to up to 50 percent of the sun's rays because of the reflective properties of the sand and water. After swimming, sit in the shade for a while—and reapply a protective lotion every hour or two.

Sunscreen and sunblock aren't just for the beach, however. Anyone living an active outdoor life should always use sunscreen. For example, skiers are exposed to sunburn twice as much due to the thinner atmosphere at high altitudes and the fact that snow is a great reflector of ultraviolet rays. For the most protection, apply sunscreen frequently. Make sure to use a sunblock on supersensitive areas like your nose and lips. Sun-protection products containing zinc oxide or titanium oxide provide almost complete protection from the sun and its ultraviolet rays.

Other methods for protecting your skin include specially manufactured clothing with sun protection built in. If you're involved in outdoor sports—for example, you're a lifeguard, a soccer player, or a tennis player—you should check out some of these products.

If you protect your skin in your teens, you'll enjoy the results as you mature. Taking care of your skin will give you a feeling of being in charge of your appearance, and that builds confidence.

ACNE: HELP!

There comes a stage in adolescence when many boys develop skin problems—the dreaded acne phase. It is a sad fact of life that acne usually hits at a time when self-confidence is at its lowest level. If one or both of your parents suffered from serious acne problems, then you are likely to have the same type of skin, but don't lose hope. There is help out there in the form of acne-fighting products, many containing benzoyl peroxide, which helps kill the bacteria and remove excess oil from the pores. Whatever product you choose, try not to become too reliant on it by using it every day. Most acne products work most effectively when used for a limited time, especially on severe acne flare-ups. Be sure to read the instructions for a particular product carefully. (If in doubt, you can ask the pharmacist at your drugstore for advice.)

Keep your skin clean by washing with a mild medicated soap, and *never, ever* pick at spots since this can cause infection and scarring. Stay away from greasy foods, which will only worsen acne. Eat lots of fresh fruits and vegetables instead. Make sure you get enough sleep, but stay active during the day and have a positive attitude. Being anxious or depressed is likely to make your skin react badly. Try not to dwell on your skin problems; instead, focus on things that make you happy, such as sports and hobbies. Remember, this is only a phase that is aggravated by the hormonal changes going on in your body, and the good news is that phases pass!

But what do you do when spots flare up just before a party or a special date? In this case a little immediate action is required. Begin to treat the acne flare-up a few days before the special event, and on the morning of the special day, cover the spots with a medicated concealing cream that blends in with your skin tone. Just cover the spots lightly—too much concealer will make the condition look worse.

In the end, you will not be the only teen with a few spots on his face, so go ahead and do the things you enjoy. If your acne is particularly severe and resistant to treatment, you may want to make an appointment to see a dermatologist.

CHAPTER 3

THE IMPORTANCE OF THANK YOU

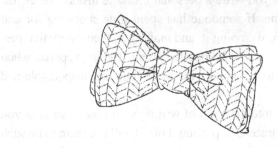

It's always nice when people give you gifts or do something nice for you. In these cases, a handwritten note of thanks in recognition of someone's thoughtfulness and generosity is in order. In my opinion, while sending a thank-you via e-mail is acceptable, a handwritten note is always more meaningful, and it is often more appreciated by the older generation who were not brought up during a time when e-mail existed. A text, e-mail, or a phone call expressing gratitude is better than no response at all, but writing a personal note shows maturity and is always a charming thing to do.

A good way to start is to buy a box of stationery with matching envelopes at any drugstore or supermarket, perhaps something in your favorite color or decorated with your initial. Another option is to buy printed thank-you cards, and that is fine as long as you write a personal message inside. Never just sign your name. If someone has spent time shopping for and selecting a gift, wrapping it, and mailing it, then surely that person deserves a warm acknowledgment. Being prepared when it comes time to say thank you makes you feel responsible and grown up.

If you get into the habit of writing your note as soon as you receive a gift, instead of putting it off, it will not seem to be such a chore. This is important, too, because the person who sent you the gift will want to know whether it arrived on time, was lost in the mail, and, most importantly, if you enjoyed it. Not sending a thank-you leaves these questions unanswered and can leave the gift giver annoyed and with hurt feelings. Taking responsibility for expressing your gratitude will please those who have gone out their way for you, and it will make your parents very proud and happy that it is one less thing they have to remind you to do.

If your parents give you a special birthday party, someone should be responsible for making sure all the gift tags are secured with extra tape so that you can write a note soon after the party and thank the appropriate person for each gift. (A younger brother might enjoy that small duty.) If there are a lot of people and a lot of gifts, sometimes it can be hard to remember who gave what. Another way to keep track is to write a list of gifts, with the name of the giver written next to each, so that you can respond with your thanks shortly after the event.

But what should you say, other than "thank you"? Don't worry. Thank you notes need not be long. Simple and sincere is the way to go. Here is an example:

EXAMPLE #1:

June 3, 2017

Dear Uncle Mike,

I had kind of a tough day at school today, but when I got home and found something in the mail for me—a package from you—it was a nice surprise and a real treat! How did you know I needed a new baseball mitt? It is going to make my summer. Thank you VERY much, and I hope to see you soon.

Love,
Billy

If you receive money, you should mention the amount and explain how you plan to spend it in your letter. For example, if you're going to deposit the money in the bank and save it for a future vacation or expensive piece of equipment, you should mention this.

EXAMPLE #2:

April 22, 2017

Dear Gran,

Thank you so much for the very generous gift of 40 dollars. It is going immediately into my savings account since I am saving for a new bike. I can't tell you how pleased I was to receive it.

I am looking forward to seeing you during the school holidays and showing you what I bought with the thoughtful birthday money.

Thanks again and I look forward to seeing you soon.

Love,
Joe

One instance when it's especially important to write a thank-you letter is after a job interview, whether it's for a summer job or your first full-time job after graduation. For more information about this, as well as a sample letter, see the "Interviewing for a Job" section in chapter 5.

There are other occasions when a written note is appreciated, such as good news—for instance, graduations and weddings—as well not-so-happy news like an illness or death in the family. A kind note at those times really helps the other person feel that someone is thinking of them, which in turn lifts their spirits.

If you make it a priority to write thank-you notes, you will soon notice how people recognize your efforts. They will think of you as a mature and considerate young person who will go far in life.

CHAPTER 4

GETTING ALONG WITH PARENTS AND SIBLINGS

You may take it for granted that your parents feed, clothe, educate, and love you, but you shouldn't. At the very least, please acknowledge your parents' existence, and better yet, show them love and appreciation in return. Simple things like cheerfulness, consideration, and a hug here and there will bring many favors your way, which is a good thing. Do your share of the chores, and don't wait to be told (or nagged) if there is a specific job you should take care of on a regular basis, like cleaning your room.

While you may feel misunderstood and resent being told what to do, it's only fair that your parents make the rules of the house—the house does belong to them, after all. In a household with people of different ages and different likes and dislikes, rules help make things run smoothly. But what about when they don't? The solution is for everyone to communicate with one another.

When arguments flare up over issues like what chores you are responsible for, sit down and discuss it quietly. Try not to show your temper at the slightest hint of parental control. Create a good impression by making a list of things your parents need you to do and promise you will stick to it without being asked. You will be treated with more respect and given more liberties by being reasonable. What goes around comes around.

Even beyond times of conflict, families need to talk and know what is going on in one another's lives. This does not mean you have to talk about every deep or private thought—you can just let your family know what is happening at school and on a social level with friends. Find the time to sit down with one of your parents or a brother or sister and just talk once in a while. One of the most frustrating things parents have to deal with is a silent teenager. I have seen adults try to have a conversation with a teen, and it is annoying when the only response is a rude "not much" or "whatever," accompanied by a shrug. If your parents are asking about your day, it means that they care, so it would be respectful to give them your full attention once in a while. It is also important for parents to understand that the time spent listening to you is valuable, too.

BEING SENSITIVE TO OTHERS' FEELINGS

While most teenagers go through mood swings and phases of insecurity, when it's happening to you, it can feel like you're the only one in the world who has felt that way. However, you are not alone. At times you would like to be left to your own thoughts and just chill, and that is your right. Remember that everyone, even adults, has good days and bad days, and you should try to be aware of their moods as well as your own. If your mother seems to have had a stressful day, or your sister quarreled with her best friend, that might be a good time to lie low in your room. On the other hand, it would be really thoughtful for you to say something encouraging, like "is there anything I can do for you right now?" Being sensitive to those around you, friends *and* relatives, has its benefits: it is the first step toward becoming a mature young person, and it will help you down the road in your adult relationships and your career.

Not to mention, it's always good to treat people with kindness. When you are down, it sure feels good to have someone be nice to you, doesn't it?

SHARING THE BATHROOM

Having to share a bathroom with a brother, sister, or other family member can be difficult, so everyone needs to be as considerate as possible to avoid conflict. The following are just a few basic rules for you to remember; I'm sure you will discover other ways to keep the peace as time goes on.

- Always put the toilet seat down and close the lid before leaving the bathroom.

- Never leave wet towels, swimsuits, or clothes on the floor.

- Rinse out the sink when you have finished using it so it is fresh for the next person. No one wants to use a sink coated with someone else's leftover toothpaste or soap!

- If there's no toilet paper left on the roll, *replace it*.

- Keep your toothpaste tube and toothbrush in a glass or holder away from everyone else's.

- Be ready to allow a family member whose need maybe greater than yours into the bathroom!

SHARING A BEDROOM

In most households with brothers and sisters, sharing bedrooms is common. Believe it or not, it has its advantages if you can work through the lack of privacy. It often brings closeness and a lifelong friendship between siblings, and sharing space with another person will teach you to get along with others and hopefully make you more tolerant of people's differences. (Not to mention, if you end up going away to college, this is excellent practice for sharing a dorm room with several other boys.)

On the other hand, it can lead to everlasting fights. Two important words to remember are *communicate* and *negotiate*. If something is bugging you about another person's personal habits (or if you seem to be annoying to someone else), take time to sit down and discuss the problem. Just as your parents have rules regarding behavior in the house, there is nothing wrong with you and your sibling making up your own rules about sharing your room. This will teach you skills for working through difficult situations and give you a strong feeling of confidence in your own abilities. Also your parents will be impressed that you have maturely figured out, and then ironed out, a problem on your own.

Being a member of a loving family is one of the greatest gifts you can receive, but everyone in the family needs to make an effort in order for things to run smoothly and harmoniously. Remember, your parents love you, but living with a teenager can be one of the hardest phases of life they go through. Try your best to make this time a good one for everyone.

BASIC RULES FOR LIVING IN HARMONY

- Say "please" and "thank you." Your parents taught you this as a baby, so for their sake, please say it.

- Abide by the rules of the house. It might be convenient to say you forgot them, but you know what they are.

- Maintain basic hygiene, including a clean face and body, and clean fingernails. Wear deodorant every day, and keep your hair neat.

- Practice good table manners (see chapter 1).

- Never talk back to your parents or use bad language.

- Strive to improve yourself. Self-improvement is the first step toward liking yourself and building character, and it will make your parents proud.

CHAPTER 5

CREATING A GOOD FIRST IMPRESSION

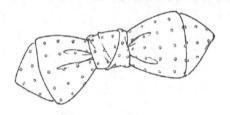

Statistics show that when you meet people for the first time, you'll make an impression on them within the first few moments. People will either like what they see and hear or not—and that could be the end of a first date or a job or college interview. So creating a good first impression is key. Fortunately, this is easy once you remember a few simple rules.

INTRODUCTIONS

Making introductions and shaking hands are polite, well-mannered things to do, but whether you are introducing yourself or being introduced to another person, an introduction should be friendly and easy. It is an immediate look at who you are. If you meet someone, and he does not look you in the eyes, does not offer to shake hands, and does not have a well-groomed appearance, you most likely will not be eager to get to know him. Don't be like him. Instead, smile, offer your hand, and say your name. When shaking hands, grasp the other person's hand firmly, but not too hard. You are simply making a friendly connection with someone—not trying to hurt them! Your clothes should be clean, your fingernails should be clean, and your hair should be brushed. Always look directly at people and be ready to say something friendly. A smiling, cheerful person who has thought about his appearance will be someone who is admired and appreciated.

Introducing yourself is easy as long as you can remember your own name! Giving some information in addition to your name to help the person remember you ("Hi, I'm Bill, David's brother") is also helpful. Make sure to have a friendly smile while making eye contact. Now it's the other person's turn to introduce himself: "Good to meet you. I'm Mike."

If you are introducing one of your parents to a friend, the adult is given priority regarding which name is mentioned first. For example, "Uncle Bill, this is my friend John." (It is not necessary to repeat, "John, this is my uncle Bill.") Some kind of comment about the person is also a good idea; for example, "John just joined our soccer team" or "Joe and his family moved in across the street." This will help make everyone feel more comfortable and get conversations started. A good way to remember which name is given first is to think about someone being introduced to a head of state or royalty. No one would say, "Mr. Smith, I would like you to meet His Majesty." It is correct to address the older or more important person (a parent, teacher, or grandparent) and introduce the younger or less important person. When you think about it, it makes complete sense. Obviously, with friends it is not necessary to think about who is fifteen and who is sixteen. At that age, you are all equally important.

If you are introducing one person to a group of friends, don't bother to go through each and every person. Instead, just introduce the new person to the group ("Hey everyone, this is Andy, who will be staying with us for a while"—your friends will probably all say, "Hi, Andy!"), and then eventually everyone can introduce themselves individually. You'll have done your part, and that should make you feel good.

But what if you've forgotten someone's name? Yes, it's awkward, but there's nothing to do here but be honest and admit that you've had a memory lapse. It happens to everyone occasionally, so no harm done.

Social occasions can often be stressful for young people, especially when entering a room full of strangers. (Don't worry, you're not alone. Some adults find this unnerving, too.) Look around. Chances are, you will be greeted by a warm smile from someone who genuinely seems to want to get to know you. Anyone who reaches out to make another person feel relaxed and at ease—putting other people's feelings before their own—is considered charming. There are times when we have to overcome our own shyness to be kind to someone else, or to meet someone in a crowd. It never hurts to start a conversation with someone, for example, when you are choosing snacks at a food table. A simple casual remark like "This looks delicious. Have you tried any of these?" can mark the beginning of a friendship.

DRESSING THE PART AND LOOKING YOUR BEST

We all have to put on clothes in the morning; otherwise we would be arrested for public nudity! But clothing is a lot more than just a covering for our bodies. What you choose to wear is a reflection of who you are and how you want others to see you. You are sending a message to other people; it can either be

"I don't care what anyone thinks of me" or "I take pride in my appearance."

Fashion and clothing are very focused on current trends, fads, color, and style, and always have been. Dating as far back as the Stone Age, when cavemen covered themselves in blue paint, making a statement about personal individuality is timeless.

No matter what you wear, you should always present the best image of yourself, as this shows you are confident and secure. However, when you are in school, playing sports, or just having fun and doing your thing, it is not necessary to think about whether your clothes match or if they are one of the latest outfits from the mall. Knowing how to dress properly for the occasion is like any other etiquette lesson. When an important event does come along, if you know how to behave and how to put yourself together, this will be to your advantage. Learn what looks good on you and what is appropriate for each occasion. Experiment with different styles until you find something that flatters your body type, height, and coloring, and makes you feel good.

In my job as a modeling school director, one of the first lessons I gave girls looking to become professional models was to suggest they take a few moments before bed and plan what they would wear the next day. It makes life simpler to have an outfit ready to wear, and it allows you to avoid the fear of oversleeping, being tardy, or looking unprepared—especially important when a girl was heading to an early-morning audition or photo shoot the next day. Sure, you're a boy and not a model, but I believe this lesson is good for everyone. In your case, if you know you have sports practice, piano lessons, or any kind of after-school activity, have those clothes folded and easy to reach when the time comes—not piled on the floor or heaped in the closet.

With that said, I will leave it to you to make decisions on your casual, everyday clothing and focus instead on providing you with some general advice on dressing for formal occasions. It is during these special times that you should project an intelligent and courteous teenager who is comfortable with who he is.

FORMAL OCCASIONS

Whether you are attending a wedding, graduation party, family reunion, or celebration at a formal restaurant, someone will be footing the bill, so it is up to the guests to show appreciation and respect by dressing appropriately. Dress codes are in place to help *everyone* enjoy a formal occasion, and when you feel well groomed, it adds to the fun of the event.

All boys and young men look well dressed in pressed pants (*not* jeans), a long-sleeved shirt, and a tie. A jacket is a nice additional touch that also shows you are taking the party seriously. It could be a blazer or any good-looking, classic style of jacket. This is the standard outfit you can depend on for special occasions. It may sound dull, like a kind of uniform, but it also makes things much easier if you have a basic outfit ready. You can still show your individual style by choosing from the hundreds of different fabrics and colors available. It feels good to be pre-pared when you receive an exciting invitation out of the blue.

Well-polished leather shoes are also a good investment to have in your closet. Do *not* wear sneakers or flip-flops to any formal function. These belong at sporting events or on the beach, not at someone's home for a party or at a restaurant.

Depending on the climate and where you live, hats are to be worn outside and should be removed when entering any build-ing. Boys should get into the habit of removing their hats when speaking to older adults and when going into someone's home. It is different for girls, since hats are part of special outfits and can be worn everywhere. It is polite for girls to remove their hats in theaters, however, since they might block the view of someone behind them. (Remember, courtesy and respect for other people are what good manners are all about.)

HOW TO TIE A TIE

Learning to tie your tie is just like learning to tie your shoelaces: once you have mastered it, it becomes an easy routine. It is one more step toward feeling grown-up and confident. One way to learn is to ask your father, grandfather, uncle, or another adult friend to demonstrate, and then copy his movements. Don't be surprised to discover that people tie knots in different fashions. An easier knot to start out with is known as the Half Windsor, but there are many different types of knots that you can learn as you get more comfortable tying ties.

The following are some simple steps for how to tie the Half Windsor. Before you begin, button your shirt all the way to the top and pop the collar up (undoing the buttons that hold the points of your collar down, if your shirt has them).

STEP 1 Start with the wide end of the necktie on your right. Make the wide end about twelve inches longer than the narrow end.

STEP 2 Cross the wide end over the narrow end.

STEP 3 Pass the wide end underneath the narrow end.

STEP 4 Fold the long end over the narrow end.

STEP 5 Wrap the wide end behind the narrow end, and then draw it up toward your chin. The back of the tie should be facing away from you.

STEP 6 Tuck the wide end, point first, through the knot.

STEP 7 While keeping a hold on the narrow end with your right hand, draw the wide end through the knot with your left hand. Pull the wide end all the way down toward your waist.

STEP 8 Adjust the knot with your left hand, keeping your right hand on the narrow end.

STEP 9 Put your collar back down, refasten the buttons, and there you are.

But what happens if when you're finished, the narrow end of the tie is longer than the wide end? Don't worry; it's a common mistake. It just means that the wide end of the tie wasn't long enough when you started. Sometimes it takes a little trial and error to find the right length, but with some practice, it will soon become second nature.

INTERVIEWING FOR A JOB

One instance where creating a good first impression is very important is when you are interviewing for a job, whether it be delivering newspapers or working part-time at a local store after school. Anyone who is considering hiring someone usually looks for qualities that will maintain the standard of their particular environment. A clean, neat appearance is usually first on the list of requirements.

According to many experts and employment counselors, the person conducting the interview often makes a judgment in the first twelve seconds of meeting the applicant! If he is not impressed with what he sees, he is not likely to change his mind later on. The important thing is to make a good first impression and maintain it.

It makes sense to check your overall appearance at the outset:

- Clothes should be clean and well pressed.

- Antiperspirant/deodorant should always be used.

- Hair should be clean and brushed.

- Good posture should be maintained, while sitting, standing, and walking. Do not fidget or slouch.

Be prepared to shake hands and remain attentive to what is going on around you. Don't forget to make eye contact and smile. Your voice is important, too. Take a deep breath, which will help calm your nerves so you can speak slowly, answering questions directly and pleasantly. By listening to what is being said to you, you'll be letting the interviewer know that you will listen to job instructions carefully.

When the interview is over, thank the person, shake hands, and leave, being careful to close the door quietly behind you. If you leave without a clatter and a bang, you are on your way to creating a very good first impression.

After you get home, sit down right away to write the interviewer a thank-you note. (If it's not possible to do so immediately, try to within twenty-four hours.) This is a must. It will create a good impression, reinforce your interest in the job, and keep you in the interviewer's mind as a good candidate.

It's preferable to send out a handwritten note in this case, but if time is of the essence, an e-mail is okay. The following is a sample post-interview thank-you note:

May 23, 2017

Dear Mr. Smith,

Thank you for meeting with me yesterday about the cashier position at Smith's Mercantile. The tour was extremely interesting, and I enjoyed speaking with you as well as your employees.

The job seems to be a very good match for my skills, most especially my assertiveness and experience working with the public. My organizational skills will be put to good use in *keeping the sales floor and merchandise neat and presentable.*

I appreciate the time you took to interview me. I am very interested in the position, and I look forward to hearing from you.

Sincerely,
Jake Turner

As you get older, sending handwritten notes of thanks will be important in your career, no matter what profession you end up pursuing, so start the habit while you are young. Although this book is written with a view to helping teenagers, many young men and women in their twenties and thirties could benefit from this advice, too.

GOING OUT ON A DATE

The time is right (you are of age and have your parents' permission), and you're considering asking that nice girl from math class out on a date. But you're not sure. Does she like you? It is reassuring to hear that someone has an interest in you, but there's no way to know for certain. So if you like someone, go ahead and ask. My advice is to try to spend time with someone and get to know her a little before embarking on a special "two-some" date. Hanging out between classes, maybe on a lunch break, is helpful to get to know about her interests and hobbies, and also look for things you might have in common. Another way is to spend time with her in a group of friends. A day at a sports event or a movie with another couple is a great way to learn how to get along with people and also takes the edge off the shyness factor.

Once you have an idea of the type of activity you would like to plan—such as a movie, concert, or barbecue with your family—then you'll know your budget. You may have to take on a couple of extra chores to pay for the date! Traditionally, the person who does the asking does the paying, so make sure you have the funds available if you want to take a girl to an expensive concert or show. (Also try to find out first if she is into that type of event.) If you build a friendship and plan other dates in the future, you might agree to go dutch sometimes.

It is important to ask a girl a few days (or maybe a week) in advance. No one likes having things sprung on them at the last minute (and she could already have other plans). Being asked out in advance gives her time to get permission from her parents and think about what she wants to wear.

She said yes. Great! But now what? The type of date you are planning—casual, sporty, a school dance, etc.—will determine what clothes you'll wear. No matter what, make sure your appearance is the best it can be, and wear clothes that will make you feel confident and happy.

If you aren't driving yet, your parents will be involved with your plans, so take that into consideration. If you are meeting the girl's parents, remember what you have read so far regarding making a good first impression, including having a friendly attitude and clean appearance, being ready to shake hands, and making eye contact. If there is a set time for the girl to be home, make absolutely sure you stick to the plan.

Be considerate and do your best to help your date have a good time. The best advice I can give is to try to have lots of things to talk about. This will help you both feel at ease and more relaxed. Discussing your tastes in music or sports is a great way to start a conversation. Don't wander off if you see your buddies or spend time talking on your cell phone—give her your full attention and keep the date lighthearted and cheerful. Have a good sense of humor. Your job is to make it a good experience for both of you.

It is good manners for a young man to walk on the "outside" (in other words, closest to the roadway) when walking along the sidewalk with a young woman. This custom began centuries ago to protect the lady from the dust and splashes of horse-drawn carriages, in the same way that handshakes originated in order to assure fellow travelers that you were not carrying a weapon. It is also good manners for a man to open the car door for a woman and offer his hand to assist her in getting out, as well as to hold the door of a building open for a woman and allow her to walk through first. Doing so will show that you are considerate, and girls love to be treated this way.

Sometimes dates don't always work out, especially when two people spend a few hours together. That's okay—it is not necessarily your fault when things go wrong, so don't put yourself down if the date is a flop. Make the best of the time, and realize you have, at least, learned what it is like to ask someone out and made every effort to make the experience a good one. If you made the girl feel special and protected, you'll have established a reputation of being someone who is fun to be with and super cool, regardless of whether or not there is a second date. And who knows—the next date you have could be fantastic!

Meeting people and learning how to get along is an important part of growing up. Try to be outgoing and friendly to everyone. You will be surprised how many friendships you make along the way.

CHAPTER 6

TELEPHONE AND
TECHNOLOGY ETIQUETTE

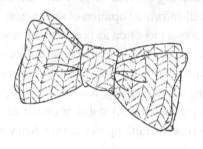

Cell phones, texting, e-mail, and the Internet make social contact immediate and, in most cases, wonderfully convenient. Unfortunately, there have not been many rules or guidelines on good manners to accompany these high-tech capabilities.

Technology enables people to build an invisible wall around them, which can be annoying to those in the immediate vicinity. It is important to realize how rude it is to ignore someone you're with in order to speak to or interact with someone who isn't even there. It's also annoying for the people you're not with—they don't appreciate your phone conversation interrupting their time.

Don't forget, condensed text messages and phone conversations can't replace meeting face-to-face. Seeing someone in person helps to build a more meaningful relationship and gives you an understanding of what he is really like, enabling you to have a more well-informed opinion of that person. Making face-to-face social contact as often as possible will also help you become a well-rounded person, rather than someone whose only interactions with people are linked to a cell phone or computer. Communicating via technology has its time and place—such as when families are in different states or countries, or when traveling—but do your socializing in person when you can.

CELL PHONES AND LANDLINES

I suggest that we bring back into our vocabulary a very simple phrase: "Excuse me." The use of these two words would be a good beginning toward eliminating much of the rudeness that often surrounds cell phone use.

Being forced to listen to loud conversations in public is annoying, so be aware of your surroundings and proximity to other people when using your cell phone. It may seem extreme, but turn your technology toys off (or at the very least, turn the sound off) when you are directly engaged with someone else. This will make a very good impression. You should make this a habit when with adults, at a job interview, in church, in someone's home for dinner, or at a concert or movie.

But what if you're expecting an important call, such as from your parents? This is where "excuse me" comes in. Say those two magic words, and then remove yourself to a more private area to quickly and quietly take the call (or, better yet, explain to the caller that you are unable to talk at the moment and promise to call back later).

When using your family's landline, there are times when a polite and courteous way of speaking is important. For example, if you are calling a friend at his home and someone in the family answers, don't subject that person to an abrupt "Is Mark there?" The person who picks up the telephone has the right to expect a pleasant-sounding voice identifying who is calling. A courteous and friendly "Hello, this is Paul; is Mark at home, please?" is always good form. Avoid calling at dinnertime or after nine o'clock at night.

When someone calls your home to ask for another member of the family, never just slam the telephone down on the counter and yell for that person. Instead, politely say, "Hold on, please, I'll get him." Put the phone down gently, and then walk away to notify the person that he has a call.

Many households and businesses have answering machines or voice mail to take messages for them when they are out. Most outgoing messages will name the person who is unavailable and sometimes give short instructions. Listen carefully to the message and wait for the signal before you speak. Speak slowly and clearly, and behave calmly, giving your name, phone number, and the reason for your call.

TEXTS, E-MAILS, AND IMS

Sending texts, e-mails, and instant messages can be quick and convenient, but it's difficult for people to get their feelings across, and things can easily be misunderstood. It can be hard to determine someone's tone in a written message: is the person joking or being sarcastic, or can you take what he's saying at face value? Because of this, we have to be careful how we word things. Sometimes discussing things in person or over the telephone helps save confusion and hurt feelings. And meeting up with friends one-on-one will improve your communication skills and confidence anyway.

I suggest you use instant messaging a little less and try to meet up with your friends on a personal level more often. This may not be popular advice, but sometimes it's cool to do things differently. Consider getting together with friends and catching up while walking, running, or cycling. An added bonus is that it will help you stay in shape.

KEEPING IT COOL ON FACEBOOK

Any type of social networking can encourage feelings of community and belonging in a positive way, particularly for a well-adjusted, confident teenager. However, researchers are now studying the effects of overuse of the online site Facebook. Parents as well as teens should know that there is some potential for harm in interacting with any social media network.

For example, if you're a teen who is feeling down, unpopular, or just plain miserable, it might not cheer you up to see a picture of a group of your friends having a good time without you. If you're suffering from low self-esteem, it may be hard to view all the updates and photos of happy-looking friends. But, let's face it. Some of those good times may be a little fake since some people like to use Facebook as an opportunity to show off, so try not to feel left out or unimportant.

You should also consider the consequences of having all your activities up on a website for everyone to look at. In some cases this could open you up to harassment and bullying, which no one needs to experience. And even if your privacy settings are at the maximum, what you share on the Internet is everlasting. What may seem fun and harmless now at your young age could come back to haunt you later, when applying to colleges and for jobs. Keep your posts classy, keep them clean, and keep personal details to a minimum. If it's not something you'd want your grandmother to see, then don't post it.

Chances are, your parents have at the very least discussed with you the amount of time you spend looking at a screen, or perhaps they've even set rules about when and for how long you're able to access social media and other technologies. You may not like this, but they have made these rules because they care about you. Older generations spent much more of their free time outdoors, which is healthier than staying inside all day surfing the Internet, watching television, and/or playing video games. Young people today are very smart and extremely intelligent when it comes to technology, which is wonderful as long as they keep it balanced with other activities, such as sports, spending time with friends, or being involved in other groups.

CHAPTER 7

NUTRITION, EXERCISE, AND HEALTH

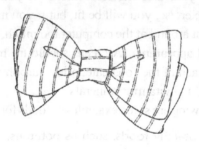

YOU ARE WHAT YOU EAT

A fit, athletic body can be achieved through following a regular exercise routine and learning the basics of healthy eating. Even just understanding the benefits of choosing fresh food instead of junk food is a great start. It seems that newspaper articles and stories on television are constantly talking about the bad effects of overprocessed foods, white sugar, salt, and junk food, as well as additives and chemicals. You may think, *But they taste good. What's so wrong with them?*

Our bodies are made up of very small units called cells, which are made up of chemicals. We use these up every second of the day as we go about our lives, walking, working, talking, and exercising. These chemicals need to be replenished, and this is where your diet choices come in. If you make healthy choices and exercise, you will be fit, but if you make unhealthy choices and sit around at the computer too much, it will show in your physical appearance. All teens should try to balance their intake from each of the food categories: carbohydrates (carbs), proteins, fats, and vitamins/minerals.

The following are some examples of foods for each category:

- **Carbs:** Starchy foods, such as potatoes, bread, cereals, and sugar.

- **Proteins:** Cheese, eggs, meat, milk, and fish.

- **Fats:** Butter, spreads, and oil.

- **Vitamins/minerals:** Iron and calcium.

If you stock up on carbs and fats, you will gain weight. It's a simple fact. However, *balance is key*. The body needs carbs and fats since they produce energy, so don't cut them out of your diet completely. Maintain a balance of all the food groups to eat healthily. Moderation and portion control are key. (For example, a serving of meat or chicken should be the size of the palm of your hand.)

Proteins are needed for growth replacement, which is essential for teenagers, and vitamins and minerals (often found in fruit and vegetables) help maintain the balance of the chemicals in our bodies.

We are what we eat, and a nutritious diet will make you feel great, with lots of energy, which will help you to look your very best. Overprocessed foods, white sugar, salt, additives, dyes, and chemicals will make you feel sluggish and run-down.

Here are some suggestions and guidelines for healthy eating:

- Eat fresh food whenever possible and avoid processed/refined foods.

- Avoid cookies, cakes, and desserts if you feel you are gaining weight.

- Eat food rich in fiber, like fruit and vegetables, to naturally cleanse the body.

- Eat less fatty and fried food whenever possible.

- Keep meal portions small, but eat enough to stay healthy and energized.

- Avoid drinking sodas; stick with water instead.

- Allow enough time for a light and energizing breakfast each morning. Your blood sugar is way down after sleeping six or eight hours, so you must boost it up if you want to avoid craving junk food later in the day.

THE ABCs OF VITAMINS AND MINERALS

Vitamins and minerals are essential to our well-being. Vitamins regulate metabolism (how our bodies process food) and energy. Vitamins A, D, E, K, and beta-carotene are fat-soluble vitamins, while vitamin C and folic acid are water soluble. On the other hand, minerals—such as calcium, sodium, magnesium, and iron—are important in varying degrees for the proper composition of body fluids.

Vitamin A is the number one vitamin for the skin. Dermatologists often prescribe it for skin problems. It also promotes good eyesight. Vitamin A can be found in carrots, cheese, sweet potatoes, squash, broccoli, eggs, and milk.

Vitamin B is said to nourish the skin and soothe away tension lines. It also helps to prevent excessive oiliness that is often a problem for teenagers. Vitamin B can be found in beef, bananas, blackberries, strawberries, soybeans, and pecans.

Vitamin C is needed for the formation of connective tissue in skin. It fights bacterial infection, aids in healing wounds, and helps to clear up bruises. Vitamin C can be found in all fruits and vegetables.

Iron is an extremely important mineral that is used in the production of blood cells. It also boosts the immune system to fight colds and other inflammatory illnesses.

Calcium, also a mineral, is necessary for the development of healthy bones and teeth. It is also beneficial for the nervous system and building muscle.

Generally speaking, teenagers should not need to take nutritional supplements—their diets should include all the necessary nutrient categories. For this very reason, it is important to learn the various food types and their values. If you and your parents, together with your doctor, decide that you need extra vitamins, be sure to read the labels of supplements carefully and take only the recommended dosage. More is not necessarily better when it comes to vitamins and minerals. Just as a vitamin deficiency can be unhealthy, too much of any one vitamin can cause problems.

You really are what you eat. A healthy, balanced, and nutritious diet will make you feel great and look your best inside and out.

MOVE IT OR LOSE IT

Exercise increases oxygen to the bloodstream, promotes better circulation, firms muscles, and provides flexibility to the body. However, for exercise to have an effect, it must become part of your daily schedule. And exercise alone will not make you lose weight—it has to be combined with a healthy diet.

Most teenage boys are active at school with P.E., as well with other activities such as soccer, hockey, football, swimming, baseball, and so on. Add to this your own personal exercise program, like running, weight training, stretching, and toning, to help you maintain an athletic physique you will be proud of. You can accomplish anything you set your mind to!

DON'T BE A DOPE

Drugs and alcohol affect the parts of your brain that control reason and judgment, as well as eyesight and inhibitions. Some young people may think that drugs, alcohol, and cigarettes make them appear grown up and "cool." They don't. While teenagers often experiment with substances in order to be accepted by a particular group, never let yourself be pressured to do anything that you feel is wrong. You have the right to refuse to join in any activity that makes you feel worried or concerned, and real friends will respect that. You should avoid the ones who don't.

Smoking cigarettes is the easiest habit to get into and one of the most difficult to stop. (Just ask any adult who smokes. Chances are, he or she has tried to quit at least once.) Smoking is damaging to your lungs, causes bad breath, stains your teeth, and will eventually affect your appearance in a negative way. (Wrinkles and yellow teeth and fingers don't look good on anyone.) It is also very expensive and could take quite a chunk out of your allowance or the money you earn at your after-school job.

If you learn at an early age about the negative effects of

drugs on your health and appearance, you will not be tempted to use them. This will help you feel more confident about your decisions.

ALCOHOL

In the United States, the legal drinking age is twenty-one, but you're still a teenager—so why even include this section in the book? Let's be realistic. It may not be legal, but some teens still drink alcohol.

When you are of legal age to drink, you will, of course, take the responsibilities that come along with this seriously. You will enjoy a glass of wine with a good meal or a glass of champagne at a festive occasion knowing your limits, and you will never drink and drive. If alcohol becomes a significant part of your life, however, it is a problem. Many adults end up being faced with this, and if you choose to drink as a teen, you could be, too. If school classes are missed, routines are disrupted, and grades begin to fall, it is likely that alcohol is beginning to take over a person's life. It's not worth the risk, and you have your whole life ahead of you.

Alcohol can affect vision and coordination, so if you love sports and competitive outdoor activities, drinking is not for you. Alcohol is filled with carbs and can lead to weight gain, so if you are concerned about your healthy lifestyle and your appearance, drinking is not for you. It becomes an especially serious factor when combined with driving. While teens are learning to drive and are gearing up to get their driver's license, they are also working on honing their judgment and reflexes. This takes time and practice, even when alcohol isn't part of the equation. All it takes is a split second of misjudgment to make the difference between life and death. Add alcohol, and that becomes more likely. A great number of driving deaths and fatal accidents involving teens are often alcohol related.

So what should you do if you go to a party where alcohol is served? Make sure you *always* leave with someone who has not been drinking. If in doubt, it is far wiser to stay where you are and have someone else pick you up later. The important thing is that you get home alive.

If you're driving, it is your moral obligation *not* to drink. If you drink and drive, you are not only putting yourself in danger; you are also endangering your passengers and anyone else who is on the road with you. It doesn't get much more uncool than that.

DRUGS

Drugs can produce dangerous changes in your mental and physical condition, including scary and violent swings in personality and perception. Some can cause hallucinations, fits, and in some cases even death. Marijuana, amphetamines, barbiturates, cocaine, and many other drugs are all highly dangerous, addictive, and illegal. People who are addicted crave the drug and will do almost anything to get it, sometimes leading to illegal or unethical behavior. Never be persuaded that a drug is "harmless." They are all harmful, even over-the-counter (OTC) medications.

Teens abusing legal substances to get high is nothing new, but the trend is worsening. DXM (dextromethorphan), a common ingredient in many OTC cough medications, can lead to drug abuse problems in the future. Research from the Partnership for a Drug-Free America indicates that teens who have abused OTC drugs or DXM are more likely to move on to illicit drugs such as Ecstasy or marijuana. Fortunately, when children are taught at an early age about the dangers of drugs, they are 50 percent less likely to try drugs when they get older.

When you look back on your teen years, you should have the happiest memories of fun with friends and family, great hobbies, sports, learning, and succeeding. It would be sad if those years were wasted on harmful substances. Stay in charge of your mental condition, your body, and your health. Only *you* can make the right decisions concerning your future.

IN CONCLUSION...

My hope in writing this book is for teenage boys to benefit from learning how to make the best impression on other people. Simply understanding the importance of presenting a friendly, polite, and well-groomed image will help everyone reach their greatest potential.

Knowing you have put your best foot forward is the first step toward building confidence and self-esteem, which will help you in all areas of life, now and in the future.

ABOUT THE AUTHOR

Wynne Dalley has an established reputation as a model agent, modeling school director/owner, lecturer, and beauty writer. Her high ethical standards in her training of students, both girls and boys, has prepared them for all careers, including professional modeling. She has lectured extensively at high schools and to teen-related groups on the importance of good manners and personal appearance, and she has dedicated her career to helping teenagers build self-esteem and confidence. Wynne Dalley is also the author of *Be Cool & Confident: A Guide for Girls.* She lives in California.